Frank Alvarado Madrigal

PITIRRE DOES NOT WANT TO SPEAK ENGLISH

Illustrated by Alicia Núñez

Drama

Order this book online at www.trafford.com
or email orders@trafford.com

Most Trafford titles are also available at major online book retailers.

Printed in the United States of America.

ISBN: 978-1-4269-3960-0 (sc)
ISBN: 978-1-4269-3962-4 (hc)

Library of Congress Control Number: 2011907038

Trafford rev. 05/25/2011

 www.trafford.com

North America & international
toll-free: 1 888 232 4444 (USA & Canada)
phone: 250 383 6864 ♦ fax: 812 355 4082

TO REMZY ALVARADO

ABOUT THE AUTHOR

Frank Alvarado Madrigal is a retired English professor in the United States. His literary work includes four poetry books that are well-known throughout Latin countries: **Simplemente tú y yo, Secretos, Añoranza,** *and "***Ensueño***". His large series of children's short stories keeps a selected corner in all libraries and bookstores around the world. A controversial political issue lived by Puerto Ricans is presented in this premium drama:* **"PITIRRE DOES NOT WANT TO SPEAK ENGLISH"**. *This first literary work as a playwright has placed Frank on top of the vertex in world literature.*

Glossary

Characters:

Mr. Pitirre	(Poet)
Mrs. Pitirre	(Housewife)
Pitirre	(Student)
Coquí	(Student)
Guaraguao	(Student)
Mr. Guaraguao	(Parent)
Mrs. Parrot	(School Principal)
Mr. Owl	(Music Teacher)
Mr. Paso Fino	(Spanish Teacher)
Miss. Eagle	(E.S.L. Teacher)
Bow Wow	(Police Officer)
Kluck Kluck	(A hen)
Pew Pew	(A chicken)
Doctor	(Character)
Sun of Borinquén	(Character)
Sea of Borinquén	(Character)
Silver Moon	(Character)
Students Choir	(Characters)

First

Act

Scene One

La Borinqueña, Puerto Rican National Anthem, is heard in the background.

Mrs. Pitirre: Wake up you, lazy creature. You are just like your father; you are always asking permission from one of your feet in order to move the other one when you walk.

Pitirre: *(Yawning)* I'm coming Mom. *(Mumbling)* Darn school! I abhor it. I still don't know why it was invented.

Mrs. Pitirre: Speak louder. I can't hear you.

Mr. Pitirre: Baby! Stop being a pain in the neck. Leave him alone. Don't you see that you might make him develop a trauma?

Mrs. Pitirre: You are going to develop one if you don't sit right away and eat your matutinal meal. I don't want to hear any complaints about breakfast being cold and don't call me baby; I'm not a baby. You, Son, shake a leg, too.

Pitirre: Daddy, don't make Mom mad.

Mr. Pitirre: *(Smiling to his wife)* Look at that! You have really stolen the show; you have made a stunning jentacular meal. Let's eat.

Mrs. Pitirre *(Looking at her husband)* It's your fault that Pitirre hasn't been arriving on time to school lately.

Mr. Pitirre: *(Surprised)* Why me?

Mrs. Pitirre: Do you still ask? You must scold him. He does not want to follow instructions, his school grades went down, and you haven't reprimanded him yet.

Mr. Pitirre: He's only failing English, Honey; he is passing the rest of the subjects.

Mrs. Pitirre: Listen to me. Why are you not embarrassed? His grades aren't scintillating to put it mildly; he has an *"F"* in English and *"D's"* in all the others.

Pitirre: *(To his father)* Bless me, Daddy.

Mr. Pitirre: God bless you, Son!

Pitirre: *(Greeting his mother)* Bless me, Mom.

Mrs. Pitirre: As usual, your father is first. God bless you, Son!

Pitirre: Mom, how come my breakfast is cold?

Mr. Pitirre: Mine, too, and my coffee is sugarless.

Mrs. Pitirre: I told both of you. Yours is *(Looking at her son)* because you sleep too much, and yours is *(Looking at her husband)* because you argue constantly.

Mr. Pitirre: True, Sweetie. Be careful! Don't burn your tongue. Your meal may be too hot.

Pitirre: *(Surprised)* How come Mom's food never gets cold?

Mr. Pitirre: *(To his son)* It does. The thing is that she does not realize it because her tongue is always hot due to her relentless talking.

Pitirre: I don't get it. Can you explain that?

Mr. Pitirre: *Shhh.* I'll explain it later; your loquacious mother is getting close. If she hears us, we won't be able to stop her verbose speech.

Mrs. Pitirre: Look at that! You both ate almost nothing. It's not worth waking up so early to fix your morning meal; you always do the same thing.

Mr. Pitirre: Come on! Don't feel bad. The problem is that you served us too much food.

Mrs. Pitirre: Yeah, right! Go and drop him off at his school, otherwise, the teachers will be calling to complain about his tardiness; I don't want to answer for something that isn't my fault.

Pitirre: *(Leaving)* Bless me, Mom.

Mrs. Pitirre: God bless you. Take care of yourself.

Mr. Pitirre: Son, I hope you haven't forgotten anything. Is everything in your backpack?

Pitirre: Yes, Daddy. Don't worry about it. Mom always puts my requisite school supplies in a day before.

Mr. Pitirre: Say! There are traffic jams everywhere today.

Pitirre: Listen, Daddy. Remember, it's Monday; Mondays are always like this.

Mr. Pitirre: *(Complaining to someone in front)* Hurry up. Hurry up.

Pitirre: Come on, Daddy. The one in front of us is an elderly. Slow down. Do not flout the traffic laws.

Mr. Pitirre: I apologize! I was not aware of it.

Scene Two

A Puerto Rican song, Lamento Borincano, is heard in the background.

Rubén Berríos Elementary School, first grade classroom, Villalba, Puerto Rico. Classrooms without air conditioned systems, of course.

Pitirre: *(Absorbed in finishing a poem about Parts of Speech and talking to himself)* I will present this poem to Ms. Eagle, so she can give me a better grade; I definitely need to improve my grade in her class.

Parts of Speech

If I decided to write a proper noun,
I would select a name such as, Mr. Brown,
but if I don't want that one, and instead,
I prefer to write a common noun,

I would choose a word such as town;
however, I may change my mind,
and write an adjective this time;
I'd choose a color such as, brown.
Let's pretend I want to write a verb
to give some action to my speech;
I would select a word such as, teach.
"An adverb", asked my friend, Coquí,
and I wrote the word, propitiously.
I'll end my poem with some prepositions
such as: along, beyond, around, and down.
If you have learned this poem as I wish,
you've learned today Parts of Speech.

Miss Eagle: Good morning class. Oh, my! It's so hot! Anyway, today's class will be about Parts of Speech…

Pitirre: *(Asking a question to his classmate, Guaraguao)* I was not paying attention. What did the teacher say?

Guaraguao: She greeted us; and then, she said that today we'll be studying Parts of Speech. She also said that she's hot today.

Pitirre: Again?

Guaraguao: Yes. She should get married.

Pitirre: I meant the subject matter.

Miss Eagle: *(Shooting a straight look at Pitirre and Guaraguao)* Are you two arguing again? That's why you both can't learn English. I want each one of your mothers to come and see me tomorrow.

Guaraguao: *(Whispering)* She probably thinks she's very pretty and wants to model for our mothers.

Miss Eagle: Who said that?

Guaraguao: Pitirre did.

Miss Eagle: Pitirre, go to the principal's office now.

Pitirre: *(Mumbling)* How in the world does she expect me to learn English if she is consistently sending me to the principal's office? She always believes Guaraguao's lies. Anyway, I don't want to learn English; I have apathy for that class. We are in Puerto Rico; we already speak Spanish, a language forcibly imposed in the past by the supremacy of a despotic power.

Mrs. Parrot: *(Inside her office, chatting over the phone to one of her very good friends)* Oh! Just a moment, please. Come on in, Pitirre. What's going on this time? Let me deduce. Miss Eagle sent you to my office because you were disrupting her class by arguing with Guaraguao, and as usual, it was not your fault. When are you going to understand that you come to school to learn and not

Frank Alvarado Madrigal

to chat with your classmates nor to remonstrate with them? It is time for you to behave with decorum. I am going to call your mother to see what we can do to surmount this persistent situation even though I don't see any immediate solution …

Pitirre: *(Whining and mumbling)* It's not fair. I'm going to quit coming to school; I want to have the freedom of flying like my father. He doesn't know English, yet nobody scolds him for that.

Mrs. Parrot: *(Dropping the phone)* Excuse me, Pitirre. Did you say something?

Pitirre: *(Still whining)* No, ma'am.

Mrs. Parrot: *(To her friend)* O.K. Hun! I think I am going to let you go; I will call you back. Let me take care of this conflict. *(To Pitirre)* It's lunch time. Go to the cafeteria, eat your lunch, come back to this office after you have eaten, and wait for me.

Mrs. Parrot leaves her office and goes to a nearby restaurant. After lunch, Pitirre waits for Mrs. Parrot's arrival. It seems that the huge amount of rice and beans that he consumed, as well as the humid and hot weather, made him sleepy. He looks around, sits on the Principal's comfortable armchair, and falls asleep. Two hours later, Mrs. Parrot steps into her office, looks at Pitirre still sleeping on the armchair, and wakes him up tenderly.

Pitirre: I don't want to speak English. I don't want to speak English. I don't want to speak English…

Mrs. Parrot: Wake up, Pitirre. That English class is driving you nuts. Let's see. Why don't you want to speak English? Explain that to me, please.

Pitirre: I am Puerto Rican, and I find the English Class abhorrent.

Mrs. Parrot: So what? I am Puerto Rican just like you; however, I learned it. Thanks to that I have had great job opportunities on and off of this island.

Pitirre: Good for you but not for me. A lot of us don't think about leaving this island because…

*I feel happy by contemplating
the white pearl sandy beaches
and listening to the waves singing
sweet and pulchritudinous songs.*

*I feel happy by contemplating
the hazel view of the sunset
and watching the sun
and the moon falling in love.*

I feel happy by contemplating
a roof full of shining stars
and under its ceiling to observe
the most beautiful place on earth.

Mrs. Parrot, with wet eyes, looks furtively at Pitirre, gently pats his back, and with a broken voice sends him to his next class.

Mrs. Parrot: *(Talking to herself)* Pitirre is right. He just made me realize all the hellacious things I have missed during my twenty years away from my island. *(A tear drops from her face and falls on top of some papers scattered on her desk.)*

Pitirre steps in his last class of the day. This is his favorite subject, not only because his good friend Coquí is there but also because it is the music class, and between his and Coquí's chant, it makes one feel that they are really symbolizing Puerto Rico.

Mr. Owl: Come on in, my dear creatures. Welcome to the world of spiritual joy where grief is forgotten, and everybody enjoys. Today we will be practicing some patriotic songs because we'll be inviting your great parents to a nonpareil and unforgettable play. You'll be the actors and will have the utmost opportunity of making them gleeful with your refined, sweet voices and unique talent.

Students Choir: *(Loud voices from avid students are heard singing enthusiastically)* **You will be precious without flags nor laureates nor glories...**

The students boisterously keep on singing all the songs that Mr. Owl, the music teacher, plays on his piano. All of them are jubilant, including Guaraguao.

Mr. Owl: Magnificent! Impressive! It's indubitable that I have the best and most precious voices of this island.

Guaraguao: Mr. Owl, why have you decorated your classroom in green and white colors? The desk, the piano, and even the wide tie you wear everyday have those colors.

Pitirre: Don't be nosey. It's Mr. Owl's classroom, and he has the prerogative to decorate it the way he wants to. I like the way it looks; those are my favorite colors.

Coquí: And mine.

Students Choir: *(At the same time)* And mine, too.

Mr. Owl: Calm down. I don't think Guaraguao had the intention to bother anyone with his question. *(The bell rings announcing the end of the school day)* On the next class, I will let you know why I adore the white and green colors. Go home and take good care of yourselves.

Scene Three

"En mi Viejo San Juan", a popular song, is heard in the background.

The Pitirres are gathered in the living room watching a baseball game on TV.

Mr. Pitirre: Look at that! That giant couldn't even hit the ball by using a guitar instead of a bat.

Mrs. Pitirre: That's why we are the way we are. As soon as the Americans discover a player that hits homeruns, he is hired by a rich team.

Pitirre: Say! Why is the one behind the batter always crouched?

Mr. Pitirre: It's a strategic position to communicate with the pitcher, and it is easier for him to catch the ball.

Mrs. Pitirre: Son, in his time, your father was an astounding player; he used to play stupendously; no ball was too difficult for him. That's how he attracted me at the beginning. Those were the good old days; they won't be back. I don't know what's wrong with me, but every time those memories show up; I get very depressed. We were so young! You were so handsome, then!

Mr. Pitirre: Look. To be languid doesn't mean to offend. What do you mean in my heyday? Get ready, Son. We will practice at the park on Sunday; you'll realize that I'm not that old. Say! Sonny, you still haven't told me how you are doing at school?

Mrs. Pitirre: Tell him, Son. Tell him that this is the third time that your teacher wants to speak with me.

Pitirre: Dad. Guaraguao disrespected the teacher by making a facetious remark, and he blamed it on me.

Mr. Pitirre: Guaraguao, again? Son, tell your teacher to sit you far away from that obdurate pupil.

Pitirre: Daddy, the teacher has done it several times; nonetheless, he keeps on moving and sitting next to me, just to irritate me.

Mr. Pitirre: I am going to have a serious talk with Mr. Guaraguao, his petulant father.

Mrs. Pitirre: No. Leave it up to me. I will solve this problem. His father has a parochial mind; he is a grunter. I know how to deal with grunters and put them in their right place.

Mr. Pitirre: That is true. It runs in the family.

Mrs. Pitirre: What are you trying to insinuate?

Mr. Pitirre: Me? Nothing.

Mrs. Pitirre: That's better. *(Looking at the kitchen's sink)* What a mountain of dirty dishes! Let's go to the kitchen to wash them. At least, you can help me by taking care of the pots and the saucepans.

Mr. Pitirre: You go first. The game will be over in a couple minutes. *(Half an hour later)* I'm here. Where are the pots and the saucepans? I don't see any dirty dishes around here; I am probably becoming blind.

Mrs. Pitirre: Say! Let me tell you the truth. You really have some audacity; you are just a lost cause.

Pitirre: *(Singing while bathing)* **What a beautiful flag! What a beautiful flag! What a beautiful flag is the Puerto Rican flag! It'll look prettier. It'll look prettier if the Yankees wouldn't...**

Mrs. Pitirre: Holy Cow! Come on. Get out of the bathroom.

Mr. Pitirre: From whom is this boy learning all those songs?

Mrs. Pitirre: From Mr. Owl, the music teacher who used to teach in Lares. His students are becoming involved by singing those types of songs.

Mr. Pitirre: A patriot has finally arrived! Look, it seems that Pitirre's food got cold.

Mrs. Pitirre: Don't start. Don't start. It was hot while he was singing in the bathroom.

Pitirre: Mom, the English teacher told us yesterday that she was going to teach us a few nice songs.

Mr. Pitirre: That is your weakness, my son. She finally hit it; she was not hitting a single one.

Mrs. Pitirre: Singing is what you do best. Changing the subject, according to the weather broadcast, it will rain all day tomorrow.

Mr. Pitirre: Wow! Good for him. He will not have to go to school tomorrow.

Mrs. Pitirre: Listen to me. Why do you say that? Do not inculcate such a bad habit to our child.

Mr. Pitirre: Hey! I can't say anything in this house anymore.

Mrs. Pitirre: It's getting late. Let's go to bed. I promised the teacher that Pitirre will no longer be late to school.

Pitirre: Bless me, Mom!

Mrs. Pitirre: God bless you, Son! Dream over me.

Mr. Pitirre: Say! Do you really want our son to have nightmares all night long?

Mrs. Pitirre: *(Looking at her husband)* You are going to sleep in your room, all by yourself, tonight. We'll see who will be having unpleasant dreams?

Mr. Pitirre: Nevermind. Forget what I've said.

Mrs. Pitirre: That's better.

The next morning:

Mr. Pitirre: I'll return home as soon as I drop him off; he's the only reason for me to go out in a rainy day.

Mrs. Pitirre: I know you hate going out when it rains; you don't need to remind me of that.

Mr. Pitirre: Don't be upset.

Mrs. Pitirre: I'm not. It's just that your passiveness exacerbates me by seeing that nothing bothers you.

Mr. Pitirre: That's not bad; it's all the opposite. I think it's extraordinary. This way, my blood pressure won't go up; otherwise, I could get a stroke or a heart attack like some individuals that are always agitated and in a hurry. Don't you agree?

Mrs. Pitirre: If you say so.

Mr. Pitirre: OK. Let's not discuss that.

Meantime, in his bedroom, Pitirre has a dream in which he shares pleasant moments among some close friends.

Sun of Borinquen: *(Singing to Silver Moon)*

So many times
I've been in love,
and I never felt
so thirsty for love.

You are the one
who makes me cry,

laugh and smile
at the same time.

Therefore sweet love
be true to me
because if you're not
I will easily die.

Therefore sweet love
be true to me,
and I will be yours
for the rest of my life.

Silver Moon: That was very sweet of you, my Dear.

Sun of Borinquen: It's has been a pleasure, Honey.

Silver Moon: There goes my answer to you, my tootsie woodsy.

Give me a hug,
give me love,
and I'll give you
what you're
looking for…

Love me once.
Love me twice.
Make my doubts
minimized.

Love me tonight.
Love me tomorrow.
Take away
all my sorrow.

Sun of Borinquén: I am stupefied..

Pitirre: So you liked the poem I composed the other day when I was at the principal's office?

Sun of Borinquén: *(Looking at Silver Moon with his eyes glooming of love)* Yes. We liked it.

Silver Moon: Tell us, how come you, being so young, are able to concoct such ravishing poems?

Pitirre: I don't know, perhaps, I inherited it from my father. I think it is just a matter of observation and sensibility.

Silver Moon: In other words, you have been observing the nice relationship between Sun of Borinquén and I. Haven't you?

Pitirre: Yes. Not only that but also the sweet way you look at each other.

Everybody looks at how Sun of Borinquén blushes; a color that could last for several hours due to his immense size. Pitirre continues dreaming and sharing.

Scene Four

A Puerto Rican song is heard in the background: **(Mulatto, look for your brown female, so you can dance Bomba, Puerto Rican Bomba...)**

Mrs. Pitirre: Son! You are all wet. Change clothes, dry your hair, and come back here, so I can give you a hot Puerto Rican soup to eat.

Pitirre: Mom, I dried my hair, but I'm still cold.

Mrs. Pitirre: Get close to me. *(She touches her son's cheeks.)* Ouch! You're boiling in fever. Take this medicine. It'll make your fever go down. Eat your soup. I cooked it just the way you like it.

Pitirre: I'm not hungry. I'm going to bed.

Mr. Pitirre: I'm here. What's for dinner? I'm starving to death.

Mrs. Pitirre: Can't you at least say, "Hi", first.

Mr. Pitirre: Hi! I'm hungry. What's for dinner?

Mrs. Pitirre: Nothing.

Mr. Pitirre: Stop joking and give me something to eat, please. I'm starving.

Mrs. Pitirre: I told you that I didn't make anything for dinner. Are you deaf?

Mr. Pitirre: Tell me, at least, what's going on. You look a little distraught.

Mrs. Pitirre: It's Pitirre. Our little son has a fever since he came home from school, and it hasn't gone down.

Mr. Pitirre: You see. I asked you not to send him to school. I'm sure he and his classmates played in the rain.

Mrs. Pitirre: Yes. I called Coquí's mother, and she told me that was exactly what they did on their way home.

Mr. Pitirre: That's why I didn't want him to attend school today. I remember when I was little; it was raining cats and dogs, and I got sick because, like our son, I also played blithely in the rain. My dad asked my mom the same thing that I requested you last night; however, she listened to him and never sent me to school during rainy days. *(He walks directly to the kitchen, finds some food, and talks to himself.)* Oh! My God! What in the world is this succulent hot soup doing in the kitchen? She told me that she didn't cook anything for supper. She's just preoccupied because Pitirre is sick; her head is all messed up. I can't understand why females are like that.

Mr. Pitirre went to take a shower after he ate the hot soup, and later, he reclined on the sofa to watch his favorite TV Programs.

Mrs. Pitirre: It seems that his fever is going down.

Mr. Pitirre: Excellent! It may just be a common cold. Say! The hot soup you prepared for me was scrumptious! You should've cooked an extra one for our son. It could resuscitate anybody; I'm sure a soup like that made *Lazarus* get up and walk again.

Mrs. Pitirre: That's not funny; you do not have any respect. That hot soup was for Pitirre. Next time you should ask before eating something.

Mr. Pitirre: All right! Please, do not get upset. The truth is that it was outstanding.

Mrs. Pitirre: Would you like me to fix you some tomorrow?

Mr. Pitirre: Would it be too much trouble?

Mrs. Pitirre: Not when you do it with love.

Mr. Pitirre: I appreciate that; I know it's a lot of work.

Mrs. Pitirre: Not really. The only thing that I have to do is open a couple cans of soups, pour them in a bowl, heat them up in the microwave for five minutes, and that's it.

Mr. Pitirre: Wait a minute. You're telling me that I ate a bowl of soup from a can, and you made a huge kerfuffle because I ate it.

Mrs. Pitirre: What? Don't tell me that you can't tell the difference between the flavor of a can soup and a home-made soup? On the other hand, you're the only one that has been aggravated around here. What's the matter with you? Did the soup make you sick? They must be out-of-date; I'll check them tomorrow.

Mr. Pitirre: I can't believe it. You fixed it for our son, and you didn't even check the due date of those cans?

Mrs. Pitirre: Listen, stop talking and let's go to bed. I have been pulling your leg; those rusty cans of soup had been inside the kitchen cabinets for more than three years.

Mr. Pitirre: I knew it. I knew it. Wait… I remember now. I bought those cans three weeks ago. No wonder the soup was so good; it was fresh.

Mrs. Pitirre: Stop being silly and let's sleep.

Scene Five

Pitirre: *(Two days after)* Mom, I'm hungry.

Mrs. Pitirre: Wow! You've finally talked! Great! You got a different face. Do you want some cereal?

Pitirre: Yes, Mom. Will Dad be arriving soon?

Mrs. Pitirre: Your daddy is here. He's taking a shower.

Pitirre: What day is today?

Mrs. Pitirre: Saturday. Why?

Pitirre: Well, Dad said that he was going to take me to the park to play baseball on Sunday.

Mrs. Pitirre: I can see that you feel better now. Do you know that you spent two days in bed? From now on, I'll follow the advice that your grandfather gave to your grandmother; I won't send you to school in a rainy day. It's incredible! Instead of going forward; we're going backwards like crabs.

Pitirre: *(Looking at his father)* Daddy, Daddy, I'm glad you're here. Look at me. I'm not sick anymore. Can we go to the park tomorrow to play baseball?

Mr. Pitirre: Yes, Son. I'm happy you're well! We are all going to the park tomorrow.

Pitirre: Mom, too?

Mr. Pitirre: Mom's invited, too. She will realize that I'm not that old.

Mrs. Pitirre: Oh, God! When that happens, I'll be the first one to know.

Pitirre: How?

Mrs. Pitirre: Nevermind. It's just business for adults.

Mr. Pitirre: Dirty mind.

Pitirre: What's a dirty mind?

Mrs. Pitirre: Nevermind. It's business for adults.

Pitirre: When will I grow up? I want to become an adult.

Mrs. Pitirre: Don't worry about it and eat your cereal.

Mr. Pitirre: If you listen to your mother, you will be feeling stronger for tomorrow.

Mrs. Pitirre: *(Talking to her husband with a low tone in her voice)* Listen. When Pitirre was sick, he was having disagreeable dreams. In his moments of delirium, he was belaboring that he did not want to speak English.

Mr. Pitirre: *(Using also a low tone in his voice)* Yes. I also heard him say a couple of times that he did not want to speak English.

Mrs. Pitirre: I better make an appointment with the psychologist.

Mr. Pitirre: *(Startled)* Are you trying to tell me that our son is crazy?

Mrs. Pitirre: Come on. What's wrong with you? A visit to a psychologist doesn't necessarily mean that our son is crazy.

Pitirre: *(Watching himself at the mirror)* It's weird! Mom said I got another face; I don't see any difference. I am bemused. It might be business for adults; I better not worry about that. (*Leaving the bathroom*) Mom, I brushed my beak. What bedtime story will you read to me tonight?

Mrs. Pitirre: Let's see. Last night, I read to you, "The Incredible Adventures of Cock-A-Doodle-Doo, the Little Rooster". Tonight, I'll be reading to you, "The Incredible Adventures of Pew Pew, the Little Chicken", and tomorrow, I'll read, "The Incredible Adventures of Kluck Kluck, the Little Hen".

Pitirre: Sounds phenomenal. Do you know that Mr. Paso Fino, the Spanish Teacher from Guayama, enjoys reading a lot of stories to our class? He has read to us: "The Incredible Adventures of Kuack Kuack, the Little Duck", "The Incredible Adventures of Bow Wow, the Little Dog", "The Incredible Adventures of Meow Meow, the Little Cat", "The Incredible Adventures of Moo Moo, the Little Cow", and "The Incredible Adventures of Baa Baa, the Little Goat".

Mrs. Pitirre: Yes, I do. I know him; he is an eminent teacher.

Mrs. Pitirre reads the story to her son. Little by little, Pitirre falls into a deep sleep. A few minutes later, she leaves her son's bedroom and finds her husband soundlessly sleeping on a comfortable sofa in the living room with the television still on.

Mrs. Pitirre: *(Talking to herself)* Oh, look at him! He got tired of waiting for me. Let me turn off the TV so he can completely rest. I've heard that if the television is on while you are sleeping, your brain doesn't rest as it should.

Second

Act

Scene One

The students are singing in the English Class.
Pollito chicken, gallina hen, ventana window…

Miss Eagle: Well! We have rehearsed enough. You have done a top notch job today; nevertheless, your homework will be to memorize all the lyrics.

The bell rings announcing the beginning of the last class.

Mr. Owl: Hello, my dear students! Today, as usual, we will be practicing songs from some well known Puerto Rican composers.

Pitirre: I love this class!

Coquí: I do, too. (*Gorgeous, melodious, and acute tones of chants are heard in the background.*) **Green light of mountain and sea, virgin island of coral…**

The bell rings announcing the end of the last class of the day.

Pitirre: *(Talking to his friend, Coquí)* It's not raining today; I think I'll go and visit my friend Pew Pew and his mother Kluck Kluck. They came from New York, and I haven't seen them in a long time. It'll be a fantastic surprise! I'd like to introduce you to them; they're very nice. Would you come with me, Coquí?

Coquí: I'm sorry, Pitirre. I have to be home on time today; my mom is waiting for me. We'll be going to visit my cousin who is sick with the flu. It's contagious; I hope not to get it from him.

Guaraguo overheard the conversation and suddenly accosted them.

Guaraguao: I'll go with you, Pitirre.

Pitirre: Oh! I didn't know you were behind us. I appreciate your offer, but I'll go by myself.

Guaraguao: *(Greatly piqued)* OK, Maybe next time.

Coquí: *(Making sure Guaraguao is not following them)* What an eavesdropper! The ubiquity of his presence vexes me.

Pitirre: Ignore him. It was just a picayune action. I'll see you tomorrow.

Coquí: See you tomorrow, Pitirre.

Pitirre headed to Kluck Kluck and Pew Pew's home. On his way, he remembers a song learned in his English Class and decides to practice it as part of the homework left by his English Teacher.

Pitirre: *(Knocking at the door)* Hi, my dear friend Pew Pew! Hello, my friend Kluck Kluck! Open the *door* or I'll get in by the *window*.

Kluck Kluck and her son Pew Pew look through the window, open the door, and hit Pitirre with a broom which makes him run away.

Mrs. Pitirre: What happened, Son? Why are you so pale? Who scared you? Wait a second. Let me answer this phone call.

Pitirre does not wait; he cries and goes to his bedroom. He does not comprehend anything.

Mrs. Pitirre: Son, open the door. Everything is copacetic. Kluck Kluck called to apologize; they did not realize it was you. They thought some crazy guy was knocking at their door saying quirky things in a funny accent, so they got scared. It's not really their fault. Just look at the way we have to live nowadays; our homes look like jails with doors and windows protected with iron bars. There is no safety; no one can be trusted. Don't worry about it. They want us to visit them anytime you like.

Mr. Pitirre: I'm here.

Mrs. Pitirre: Shh. Lower the tone of your voice. Pitirre is sleeping.

Mr. Pitirre: You seem a bit aggrieved again. What's the matter with you this time?

Mrs. Pitirre: Pitirre has a pejorative attitude; he didn't want to eat anything today. I got a phone call from Kluck Kluck, and she told me that he went to her house acting peculiar; she implied that Pitirre is crazy.

Mr. Pitirre: Oh, Lord! Please, do not wait anymore. Take him to the psychologist tomorrow. However, I didn't notice anything differently when we were at the park yesterday. How about you?

Mrs. Pitirre: Neither did I.

Mr. Pitirre: We never had this type of anomaly in my family. What about in yours?

Mrs. Pitirre: No.

Pitirre sleeps and starts dreaming about what has been happening to him after he began attending the English Class; he wakes up crying.

Pitirre: I don't want to speak English! I don't want to speak English! I don't want to speak English!

Mrs. Pitirre: Son. Son. Don't cry. It was just a nightmare. I'm going to lie down next to you, so you won't have anymore disturbing dreams.

Mr. Pitirre: That language is going to make him crazier. Let me turn on the television and watch the news. Wow! Things look chaotic in the Middle East. Nobody will draft my son; we have enough injustices on our island to take care of. That is why a few real and tenacious Puerto Ricans have waged an unremitting battle against the usurper's wonton acts and made the U.S. Air Force stop using Vieques as a bombing range because their malfeasances were creating a plethora of problems. These Puerto Rican heroes realized that pernicious foreign intervention was the harbinger for disaster. Oh, God! It's late. Let me turn off the television and go to bed, if not, I won't be able to get up tomorrow.

Mrs. Pitirre: *(At sunrise)* Listen. Wake up. Why did you sleep on the sofa last night?

Mr. Pitirre: I fell asleep waiting for you to come out from Pitirre's bedroom.

Mrs. Pitirre: Oh, God! I'm sorry. Pitirre held me tight all night long. Let me make some breakfast before he wakes up; meantime, you can take a shower.

Mr. Pitirre: *(Leaving the bathroom)* That coffee smells fabulous!

Mrs. Pitirre: Hurry up. I fixed ham and cheese omelets with bacon, toast, and orange juice.

Mr. Pitirre: Is Pitirre awake?

Mrs. Pitirre: There he is. He's coming. Talking about the devil…

Mrs. Pitirre: Pitirre, please, take a shower; I don't want you to be late for school.

Pitirre: All right. Bless me, Mom. Bless me, Dad.

Mrs. Pitirre: God bless you, Son.

Mr. Pitirre: God bless you!

Scene Two

Guaraguao: *(Strongly patting Pitirre's back)* Say! Pitirre. What's up? How come you didn't come to school yesterday?

Pitirre: If you don't stop hitting me so hard, I am going to report you to the Principal.

Guaraguao: What happened? I'm just playing.

Pitirre: Well, stop it. I am not in a mood for such perennial games.

Guaraguao: O.K. I won't do it again.

Pitirre: I hope not.

Guaraguao: Well, you still haven't answered my question.

Pitirre: Oh! I went to see a psychologist.

Guaraguao: A psychologist?

Pitirre: Yes. A psychologist.

Guaraguao: That's interesting.

Pitirre: Why did my parents take me there?

Guaraguao: Well, my friend, you probably have a loose screw.

Pitirre: I did not know that we have screws inside of our bodies?

Guaraguao: No. That's another way of saying that you are nuts; in other words, you are mentally ill.

Pitirre: *(Furiously, Pitirre attacks Guaraguao.)* You are the crazy one, not me. You are always besieging me.

Guaraguao: Ouch! Ouch! Ouch! Mrs. Parrot. Mrs. Parrot. Mrs. Parrot. Protect me. Pitirre is hitting me; he's mad.

Guaraguao precipitately runs away and goes to the principal's office to make a complaint. Pitirre flies after him confounded by Guaraguao's gratuitous remarks.

Mrs. Parrot: *(After she listens to Guaraguao's side of the story)* Tell me, Pitirre, why did you attack Guaraguao? Don't you know that he likes you a lot? Well, since you are keeping your ruminations to yourself and don't want to answer my questions, I am going to suspend you from school for three days. When you return, do not forget to bring your mother with you. Your grades are very low, and your aberrant behavior has worsened by hitting someone which constitutes a major offense. Let's see if you learn your lesson this time and do some positive changes in your life.

Pitirre walks out from the principal's office. While exiting the school, he listens to the beautiful songs that are being sung in Mr. Owl's Classroom. Silently and with tears rolling down his cheeks, Pitirre exits the school. In the distance, he can still hear one of his favorite songs.

Students Choir: *My little school, my little school, I love it very much because it's here, because it's here where we learn...*

Pitirre: *(Talking to himself and still with tears in his eyes)* I will fly to the peak of that tall mountain to admire the bucolic splendor of my island and listen to the waves of our blue sea singing in a language that I recognize and is not abstruse to understand.

Sea of Borinquén:

Pitirre, Pitirre.
Singing bird,
today, I notice
a different tone.

Pitirre, Pitirre.
¿Could it be, perhaps,
a lament for the lost
of a great love?

Pitirre, Pitirre.
Singing bird,
the grief in your echo
reaches the sun.

Pitirre, Pitirre.
Singing bird,
dry your tears and
talk to me about your pain.

Pitirre, Pitirre.
Tell me, please,
what affliction does
invade your heart?

**Pitirre, Pitirre.
Could it be, perhaps,
a lament caused
by the injustices
against your land?**

Pitirre: Dear Sea of Borinquén! How do you know? Yes, I am fed up with all the injustices committed against my island. So called conquerors came and made us adopt their customs. We have not finished learning a language from a past culture, and here we are again, forced to learn another one imposed by a different and new arriving imperialist power. That is why... *(Someone interrupts.)*

Pitirre's arrival to the peak of the mountain serendipitously coincided with that of his father.

Mr. Pitirre: Say, buddy. What are you doing here? Who are you talking to?

Pitirre: *(Perplexed)* Daddy! I did not expect to see you here. Mrs. Parrot suspended me although it was not my fault; it was Guaraguao's.

Mr. Pitirre: Do not say anymore. I am going to talk to his father. If he does not put an end to his son's undesirable behavior, I will put them in their right place.

Pitirre: Forget it, Dad. Why don't you take me to all those incomparable places where you have been. Take me to Vieques, Culebra, Cabo Rojo, Humacao, Isabela, San Lorenzo, Caguas, Arecibo, Utuado, Quebradillas, Orocovis, Morovis, Ponce, Aguadilla, Fajardo, Loiza Aldea, Piñones, San Juan, please, take me around this scenic island. I have three days off. If we count Saturday and Sunday, it'll be a total of five days. Just imagine!

Mr. Pitirre: Super! Wait a second. Are you telling me that Mrs. Parrot suspended you for three days? Well, let's go to Mayaguez and invite my brother and your dear cousins, too.

Pitirre: What about Mom? Won't she get angry?

Mr. Pitirre: No, she won't. Precisely, she is in Mayaguez, at her sister's home. She left this morning to meet your new baby cousin, so let's go there first and let her know that we'll be flying around this cozy island.

Pitirre: Let's hurry! What are we waiting for? I have an idea. It's too hot. Let's drink some coconut water first so we will not have to make a stop.

Sea of Borinquen:

I'm going up and down
as a wave on the sea.
I felt myself like a stranger
in this world.

Suddenly, I met you,
and now, I feel crazy.
Yes, I feel crazy
just for thee.

I realize that I was wrong.
I thought love did not exist.
How can I let you know
that I'm dying of love for thee?

You perhaps wonder why
this is happening to me,
but for now, I must say that
tears of love
from my heart
are falling down.

Two hours later:

Mrs. Pitirre: Say! What are you doing here? I thought you were in school, Son.

Mr. Pitirre: He was bored and wanted to take a trip.

Pitirre tells his parents everything that happened at the school; and then, he goes and plays with his cousins.

Mrs. Pitirre: (*To her husband*) Come on, Darling! I want you to try this superb rice with pigeon peas. I did not offer any to Pitirre because he prefers playing than eating. He knows he could have indigestion if he exercises after eating.

Mr. Pitirre: Stop talking and let me try this so called exceptional dish.

Mrs. Pitirre: What's the hurry? Sit down and relax. Just give me a minute.

Mr. Pitirre: *(While eating)* The truth is that your sister really knows how to cook. This dish is out of this world, and this passion fruit juice is very tasty.

Mrs. Pitirre: I knew you were going to like the rice, but wait till you try the coconut dessert I made.

Mr. Pitirre: Oh! I love it! Hurry up. Give it to me. Quick, I can't wait.

An hour later, Pitirre looks for his father everywhere; nonetheless, he cannot find him.

Pitirre: Mom, Mom. Have you seen Dad? I have been looking for him, but I can't find him.

Mrs. Pitirre: He left in a hurry about an hour ago; I thought he was with you. Look. He's coming. (*To her husband*) What kind of face is that? Where have you been? Your son has been looking for you.

Mr. Pitirre: Sitting on the toilet. I had a stomach ache and diarrhea.

Pitirre: I'm glad I did not eat that food; I would have gotten sick, too.

Mrs. Pitirre: No, Son. Your dad's meals are usually a surfeit for him; therefore, he got ill.

Mr. Pitirre: Oh, no! I am a bottomless pit. I'm hungry; my stomach is empty. Is there any rice left?

Scene Three

Pitirre: Dad, I would have liked for Mom to come with us. Wow! I always wanted to be here. I heard a lot about this exotic phosphorescent bay.

Mr. Pitirre: Your mother must be very ecstatic in Mayaguez, at her sister's house; they really enjoy being together. They talk about their children and remember everything about them. Oh! Don't worry about your Mom. She was here before you were born; in fact, it was precisely in this place where we spent our honeymoon.

Pitirre: Honeymoon? I thought the moon was made out of cheese.

Mr. Pitirre: Don't worry about it. That is...

Pitirre: *(Interrupting)* I know. That is business for adults. *(Father and son laugh at the same time.)* You must have spent an unmatched time with my mom. Do you by any chance remember a nice poem from that romantic occasion?

Mr. Pitirre: Oh! Yes, I do. Listen to this one:

There will be another day.
There will be another time.
There will be another night.
There will be another sight.

Until then, I won't give up.
Until then, I won't stop
feeling what I feel for you,
inside my heart.

And now sweet love
whisper in my ear.
Whisper what my soul
eagerly wants to hear.

Don't you see tears in my eyes?
They are saying
that without your love
I would rather die…

Pitirre: I am really impressed. No wonder my mom fell in love with the best poet of all times.

Mr. Pitirre: Thanks, Son. Let's change the subject for a second. It's a pity that your cousins are not here with us; notwithstanding, you know that my brother does not want his children to be absent from school.

Pitirre: I am lucky I'm your son and not my uncle's!

Mr. Pitirre: Let me tell you that I am not very pleased with you being out of school, yet I know it wasn't your fault. Anyhow, let's enjoy this vacation.

Pitirre: That is why I love you so much, Dad.

Mr. Pitirre: Why?

Pitirre: You are caring and understanding; you are the best dad in the whole world.

Mr. Pitirre: I also love you because you are the most considerate son in the world. Gosh! It's late! Let's go to bed now. We'll be travelling to another interesting and stunning place tomorrow. *(They hugged each other and fall asleep.)*

In the morning, Pitirre is awaked by the mellifluous chant of one of Coqui's relatives. Pitirre gets up and starts singing inspired by the magnanimous view of the phosphorescent bay.

Pitirre:

A Puerto Rican sunrise
in front of a shining mirror;
so it is the sea of Borinquén
when it reflects the rays of the sun.
So it is the land where I was born;
small but pretty.
So it is my resplendent little island:
The land of Coquí!

Mr. Pitirre: *(Wakes up amazed by the inspired euphonious chant of his son)* There is no doubt. You really love this land as much as I do; you are a true Puerto Rican.

Pitirre: Yes, Dad. I will be more than proud to give up my life for my beloved Puerto Rico, but let's not be confused, I said Puerto Rico.

Mr. Pitirre: That's my son! Let's adjust our seat belts because we are heading to Cabo Rojo. It's been a long time since I have eaten a good dish of conch.

Pitirre: I thought you were going to eat a red snapper with a side dish of ground green plantains mixed with lobster. Isn't this type of *Mofongo* your predilection?

Mr. Pitirre: I am a polyphagous individual; I don't have any difficulty eating.

Under the blue sky of the picturesque Enchanted Island, father and son fly blissfully over the green mountains and the fragrant foam made by the waves of the sparkling sea that warmly caressed the white pearled sands. Everything is felicity in this paradise!

Pitirre: Everything was divine. Where do you want us to go now?

Mr. Pitirre: Aren't you exhausted? That food really made me sleepy. What about relaxing under that glaze of color flamboyant tree?

Pitirre: I am not tired, but I know you need to rest because you overate.

Mr. Pitirre: I really feel replenished. Thanks for your understanding.

Pitirre: You are welcome. You should control your voracity. How is your blood pressure?

Mr. Pitirre: Say! What do you know about it? Who's teaching you that?

Pitirre: At school. I learned that one has to be aware of the amount of fat and sodium in all foods. Being overweight is directly connected with hypertension. Be careful! I see your belly has incredibly grown lately.

Mr. Pitirre: What else have you learned?

Pitirre: Hypertension is an illness called the silent killer because there are no symptoms in most cases. Then, all of a sudden, a stroke or a heart attack may kill you. I am not saying this to scare you. Just be careful…

Scene Four

La Borinqueña, a National Anthem composed by Puerto Ricans, is heard in the background.

The Pitirres are resting in their sweet and peaceful home.

Mrs. Pitirre: I love the way my little niece was smiling at me when I had her in my arms; anybody would have thought that she knew me already. Oh! I love her as if she were my own daughter. I'd like you to listen to a song I composed to her...

You make me feel fine;
you make me feel
like someone;
the creature I wasn't
in a long time.
You came into my life
brightening the stars
in my nights.

Frank Alvarado Madrigal

*You make me learn
who I am,
and how to stand
all the time.
Please never leave me
and I never will;
of what I'm saying
I'm very sure.*

*'Cause you're the reason
of spinning the moon
for those who are in love—
for those who have found
the very good luck
of being together
and love each other
as much as we do.*

Mr. Pitirre: Glorious! Flawless! It really came out from the bottom of your heart.

Mrs. Pitirre: Oh! Thank you, Sweetheart.

Mr. Pitirre: Honey, tomorrow is Monday, and we'll have a meeting with the School Principal; consequently, we must go to bed early tonight.

Mrs. Pitirre: Our son must be exhausted from that trip; it would have been better to stay home and help him with his school work.

Mr. Pitirre: You're correct. Especially English; he can't stand it.

Pitirre: School again! It would be more enjoyable without the English Class; most subjects are passable except for that one.

Mr. Pitirre: He had fun; that's what counts.

Pitirre: More likely, that was a good opportunity for my dad to take me to all the attractive and interesting places of this island. Just imagine! I went to Vieques where we ate a lot of small citrus fruits called cherry azaroles, rich in C Vitamin. We also went to Culebra, Juana Diaz, Comerío, Guayama, Gurabo, Manatí, Lares, and many more resplendent places. The truth is that, as my good friend wrote in one of his famous songs, I am very fortunate to be born on this land where my eyes saw the light for the first time.

Mr. Pitirre: Oh! I love his song.

Mrs. Pitirre: Sunshine, tell me why didn't you come straight home when you were suspended from school? I have told you several times to come directly here after you leave school; you are still very little to be wandering by yourself. You have watched the news on the television; you must be cognizant about the dangers out there. If anything happens to you, we will be very affected.

Pitirre: I am sorry; I will not do it again. I didn't want to make you sad by seeing me crying; that's why I did it.

Mr. Pitirre: That's O.K. Don't feel bad, Son.

Mrs. Pitirre: It is time for you to go to bed, Sweetheart. Oh, do not forget to brush your beak.

Pitirre: I won't. Good night, Mom.

Mrs. Pitirre: Good night. Sweet dreams.

Pitirre: Thanks, Mom. Good night, Dad.

Mr. Pitirre: Good night, Dear.

Mrs. Pitirre: Are you saying that you found him crying and talking to the sea? My goodness! We must tell that to the psychologist. Remember, he asked us to observe him closely and document any behavioral changes; I think we must report that. I'll make an appointment for tomorrow. Tell me what other particular things did you notice on those days that you were with him?

Mr. Pitirre: Let me think. Oh, yeah. Something else that attracted my attention was…

Mrs. Pitirre: *(Interrupting)* Shhh. Wait, he's coming. *(Talking to her son)* Honey, I thought you were already snoring.

Pitirre: Mom, I can't sleep. I didn't know I snore like Dad.

Mr. Pitirre: No, Son. What your mother said is that she thought that you were soundly sleeping.

Pitirre: How will I know the day when I will start snoring?

Mr. Pitirre: Somebody will tell you. Just don't worry about it right now.

Pitirre: I know. That is business for adults. Mom, come to bed and hug me like the other night, please.

Mr. Pitirre: Gee! I'll be spending another night on a diet, again.

Pitirre: On a diet? I saw you eating excessively a while ago.

Mrs. Pitirre: Sonny, don't worry about that.

Pitirre: O.K. It must be business for adults, I guess.

Mrs. Pitirre: That is correct. Let's go to bed.

Mr. Pitirre: *(A little later)* Is he sleeping?

Mrs. Pitirre: Yes, he is. Say! There is something else that I'd like to discuss with the psychologist.

Mr. Pitirre: What is it?

Mrs. Pitirre: Lately, Pitirre has been asking me to hug him at bedtime; otherwise, he would not be able to sleep. It makes me think that he feels insecure. Say! Don't you think it is time for us to have another baby? The other day when I had my little niece in my arms, I felt some kind of sweet maternal instincts; therefore, I wanted to ask you about making our family a little bit bigger. What do you think?

Mr. Pitirre: It is a glamorous idea, so our son will have someone to play with.

Mrs. Pitirre: I would like a female this time.

Mr. Pitirre: Whatever. A male will be fine.

Mrs. Pitirre: What do you mean? You should have seen my little niece: Her little fingers, little cheeks, little eyes, little…

While Pitirre's parents were trying to agree, their son was having a dream about the places he visited during the absent days from school. In his dream, he was delighted by watching and listening to Sun of Borinquén singing lyric songs to the Enchanted Island.

Sun of Borinquén:

I love Borinquén and its blue sea.
I love The Yunque, Coquí,
and this land that houses me.
I love Pitirre and all things
from here, and I love you,
voluptuous Puerto Rican,
for being the blithest
and most callipygous butterfly.

Pitirre: *(Talking during his dreams with some of his very close friends)* I love your eloquence; the truth is that you really know how to say nice things. Those callipygian tagfalters that were flying over the flowers are the jolliest and most captivating butterflies I have ever seen in my life.

Sea of Borinquén: No. Excuse me but I do not concur this time. If there is someone here who knows how to express himself with spontaneity and receive our accolades, it's you, Pitirre. You are a prodigy! *(To the others)* What do you think?

Silver Moon: I agree. You are the gentlest and most sensible creature I have ever known in my life; there are no words to describe all the kindness that fills your humble heart.

Coquí: We love you a lot, Pitirre. Take care of yourself because our island would not be the same without you.

Scene Five

Rubén Berríos Elementary School, Principal's Office

Mrs. Parrot: Good morning. How are The Pitirres today? It is a pleasure to have you here, so we can discuss your son's case. We need to find some strategies in order to assist him not only in his academics but also in his behavior. According to Ms. Eagle, Pitirre is having many complications in her classroom.

Mrs. Pitirre: Good morning, Mrs. Parrot. Precisely, we wanted to talk to you about that and some other issues. Our son has been acting strange; therefore, we have been taking him to a psychologist in order to find a solution. By the way, his next appointment will be tomorrow.

Mrs. Parrot: Oh, my God! This is serious. Please, keep me informed. With our support and yours, we can make Pitirre improve his performance. I will meet with Miss Eagle, his English Teacher, to let her know about this problematic situation. Do not worry about the absences, I will justify them.

Mrs. Pitirre: We appreciate your benevolent gesture. We don't know how to reciprocate for your kindness, undoubtedly, our community is very lucky by having a pivotal public servant like you.

Mrs. Parrot: Do not mention it. I am the one who is very thankful with both of you for coming and sharing all this important information. *(A big noise is heard in the school backyard.)* Oh, my God! What's that? Excuse me, please. Let me check what is going on out there. Wait for me. I'll be right back.

Students: Hit him, Pitirre. Go on Guaraguao. Hit him, Pitirre. Stand up, Guaraguao.

Mrs. Parrot: Let me through. What is going on here?

Students: Pitirre and Guaraguao are fighting because Guaraguao slandered Pitirre by spreading spurious rumors that Pitirre is cracked; moreover, he said that's why you kicked him out of the school like a dirty diaper.

Mrs. Parrot: *(Guided by the querulous voices from the students)* What do you think you're doing? This is an educational setting. Let me make very clear to all of you that this is not a boxing ring; you all attend school to learn, and that includes proper manners. To transgress rules is tantamount to school suspension. Let's go to my office, immediately. Help me out, Mr. Owl, please.

Mr. Pitirre: Son! What happened?

Mrs. Pitirre: *(Exasperated with tears in her eyes)* Tell us, Son. What's going on? You can be sure that we will understand, and we'll give you all the assistance you need; you know that we have always wanted the best for you.

Mr. Owl: Please, excuse my interruption. Mrs. Parrot, hurry up and call 911. Guaraguao is badly hurt. He is not waking up; he was knocked out. *(Looking at Pitirre's father)* Mr. Pitirre, my premise is that your son's worth a fortune. You should take him to Las Vegas; he hits like a champion. Wow! Incredible! *(Miming with his hands a boxer in action)* Left, right, left, right, one more left and finished.

Mrs. Parrot: Mr. Owl! How can you dare to make such comments? Let me remind you that you are in a school, and we fight and defeat violence with the powerful weapons of wisdom.

Mr. Owl: I'm sorry. I allowed my emotions to dominate me. Jesus! If one of those famous promoters from boxing gets to see him, he will become the world's most famous boxer

Mrs. Parrot: *(Dialing 911)* I am calling from Rubén Berríos Elementary School. Please, send an ambulance right away. I have a knocked out boxer, I mean, an unconscious student. *(Talking to Pitirre)* How do you feel? Are you O.K?

Mr. Owl: *(Talking to Pitirre)* Unbelievable! Not even a single scratch. What a lesson! It seems that you have been fed with roots. Right or left, I don't know which one is the best; you were born to be a champ.

Mrs. Parrot: Mr. Owl. Go back to your classroom and thanks for your cooperation.

Mr. Owl: You're welcome, Mrs. Parrot. What good old days when I used to box!

Mrs. Parrot: *(Talking to herself)* What am I going to do with this teacher? He is a good educator, but sometimes he behaves like a student. I wonder if that was the reason he was transferred from his previous school.

Mr. Pitirre: I beg your pardon, Mrs. Parrot, I did not hear what you just said. I was thinking about what Mr. Owl was talking about.

Mrs. Parrot: Nothing. The thing is that being a school principal is a difficult job; it is very stressful. It requires a lot of patience to deal with so much at the same time; it's really an arduous task. Let me tell you that it is not only the students; otherwise, it would be simple. School principals have to deal with teachers, parents, community leaders, politicians, and let me not continue because it is an endless story. I am just waiting for my retirement day, so I'll be able to relax; if not, I would die from a heart attack.

Mrs. Pitirre: Please, accept our sincere apologies. It has never been our intention to make your job harder than what it already is.

Mr. Pitirre: Please, let us know how we can help you. What can we do in this case? Are you going to suspend our son, again? *(An ambulance siren is approaching)*

Mrs. Parrot: Excuse me, please. Let me take care of this business.

Mr. Pitirre: *(A couple minutes later, the ambulance's siren is heard again.)* We are very sorry Mrs. Parrot; we still don't know what the cause of the fight was. Our son is reticent; he has not uttered a single word.

Mr. Parrot: It looks like Guaraguao is in a serious condition. He was taken to the Medical Center in Río Piedras; he has some kind of brain damage.

Mr. Pitirre: You are kidding!

Mrs. Pitirre: Holy Cow!

Mrs. Parrot: I have been trying to get in touch with The Guaraguaos without any success.

Mr. Pitirre: Don't you have their cellular phone number?

Mrs. Parrot: Yes. I do, but it looks that they have one of those pre-pay cellular phones, and it probably has run out of air-time. Let's go over the question you asked me related to your son before the paramedics came here. I think it's better to leave your son at home for a week; time is needed for things to settle down.

Mrs. Parrot tells The Pitirres about the extremely vexing situation on how Guaraguao was vilifying their son by making caustic comments while he was suspended from school, according to the students' stories.

Mrs. Pitirre: *(Breaks in tears)* Some creatures are cruel! Where do they learn such behavior? They probably learn it from watching television; I don't think they learn it in school.

Mrs. Parrot: I don't agree; they learn a lot of bad things at schools. The good old days are gone when the teachers had all the authority to use corporal punishment to straighten the students' behaviors. Nowadays, educators cannot even give them a look of disapproval for wrong doing; they are afraid to be sued by them or even by their parents. For many teachers, teaching is the only source of income to feed their families. It is not a secret for anyone that their salaries are an insult to the profession they love, value, and carry out with dignity. A teacher is a teacher because the need to educate and shape the future of our youngsters runs in their veins. In the final analysis, our descendents are the future of our country: of our world. There is no respect. Teachers feel handicapped; they can't express themselves because they are afraid of being punished by losing their jobs. They spend most of their time working on legal documents and teaching test materials to please their state governments. Where are the values? That is why our generations are full of philistine ignorant creatures who lack of the basic values to conduct themselves and succeed in life. What about the few parents who grew up in good ethical environments? They are afraid to discipline their youngsters knowing that a call to 911 by this new generation can put them in trouble. That is why we are the way we are. What about the television? Many homes have one in each room, so their youngsters will not fight for the remote control, or maybe because it is the easiest way for many parents to free themselves for a while. Some others use this free time to do house chores, forgetting in this way, that strict supervision is the most important chore of the house. Other parents use the time to gossip with their friends or relatives; others have a propensity to drink alcoholic beverages either by themselves or with friends. In fact, we are living a crazy world since the authority was taken away from the good parents and teachers. Remember it is not only the teacher's job to educate in order to transform and improve the future of a nation; it takes a whole community to accomplish such task. We all know that there have been cases of teachers and parents that have abused their power, but I still can say that the old disciplinary methods were better than today's. Let us not talk about gangs or drugs. Those are the two worst nightmares killing our society, but that is a separate chapter to discuss. In fact, I do not really know what the future will hold for us…

Mr. Pitirre: You are right, Mrs. Parrot. Well! We know you are very busy and have been working without respite; we really appreciate the time you courteously dedicated to us. Have a good day, Mrs. Parrot.

Mrs. Parrot: Thanks. Have a nice day, too.

Mrs. Pitirre: Let's go, Son. Good bye, Mrs. Parrot.

Mrs. Parrot: Good bye, you all.

Mrs. Parrot sends an e-mail to all the teachers asking them to join her for an after school emergency faculty meeting. She also asks them to bring all the academic documentation pertaining to the two protagonists of the fight.

Third

Act

Scene One

That afternoon at Rubén Berríos Elementary School, there was a faculty meeting in order to decide about the best educational programs for Guaraguao and Pitirre.

Mrs. Parrot: *(Broaching the subject)* Good afternoon everybody. The purpose of this meeting is to decide the best educational program for two of our students. The alternatives are a correctional facility, an academy for students with special needs, or a home study setting. On this third option, a Special Education Teacher will assist both students. The school district will provide them with a personal laptop, so they will be able to use the internet for homework purposes. I also want to emphasize to all of you that this process takes time; I call it bureaucratic procrastination. In the meantime, we will watch them closely inside the school, and the police will be watching them outside of the campus. Just remember that our students are the paramount reason for us to be here.

The faculty meeting continued its flow, obviously, in a very professional manner; all the teachers were participating by checking the students Cumulative Folders, class works, grade books, portfolios, etc. At the end, for the best interest of the students, Mrs. Parrot and the teachers agreed to place them in the Home-Bound Educational Program. All of a sudden, the faculty meeting was interrupted by a big commotion coming from the blacktop area. They all went to check what was happening. Mr. Guaraguao was in the middle of the school patio jeering and calling the school principal.

Mr. Owl: If you don't mind, Mrs. Parrot, I can teach one or two lessons to that blatant individual on how to conduct himself civilly in a school environment. My fists, I mean, my lessons in ethics will take care of his sulkiness.

Mrs. Parrot: I appreciate your offer, Mr. Owl, but I will take care of this choleric parent by myself; I know how to appease an irreverent like him. Remember, I am the principal.

Mr. Guaraguao: *(Whooping in a defiant attitude)* Where's my son? I heard he got whipped.

Mrs. Parrot: If you lower your voice, I will be able to explain your son's reprehensible act; otherwise, I will have to call Mr. Pitirre, so he can explain to you the acerbic comments done by your son against Pitirre.

Mr. Guaraguao: *(filled with trepidation and using a lower tone in his voice)* No. No. I am very sorry. Please, do not call him. Forgive me, Mrs. Parrot.

Scene Two

Mrs. Pitirre: What are we going to do? Pitirre has stopped talking, eating, singing, and watching the television programs; he is despondent. He didn't even answer the questions that his psychologist asked him. He used to be so happy! The psychologist hasn't noticed any improvement; he feels afraid that Pitirre's mental health is deteriorating. Moreover, our son still continues suffering from the same nightmares.

Mr. Pitirre: How do you know that they are the same?

Mrs. Pitirre: In his bad dreams he reiterates over and over that he does not want to speak English.

Mr. Pitirre: It could be his teacher's fault? Remember, she is not from here. It could be that she is not using the right instructional methods to teach English as a second language, and the Total Physical Response Strategies are probably so recondite that her students are not getting the message.

Mrs. Pitirre: Come on! Don't tell me that you are a racist. I don't think that being from the U.S.A. will have something to do with what is happening to our son; besides, why are his classmates able to learn English, and he is not? Pitirre has not shown any interest in that language not even by watching cartoons in English.

Mr. Pitirre: How do you know that his classmates are learning English?

Mrs. Pitirre: Well, I suppose they do. Wait a second! Now that you are mentioning it; Coquí's mother had made some comments about her son's attitude towards that language. She said that he has not learned a single word in English, and the majority of the students are reluctant to learn it; moreover, she stated that Pitirre avowed that nobody, including Ms. Eagle, has to speak English in Puerto Rico. Pitirre also has told his English Teacher to get out of our island because he is fed up of seeing so many foreigners sticking their nose in our business and trying to run our lives.

Mr. Pitirre: How come you forgot to tell me that? I got the picture now. What my son has been experiencing is a feeling of resentment, a rebellious attitude, a feeling of impotence, a frustration of knowing that he is confronting the world by himself against what he considers wrong;

his classmates are submissive to this unfair reality. Just look at Coquí's acquiescence. He would never dare to step ahead to complain even when he is right. On the other hand, Guaraguao's animosity is evident and has acquired the absurd affectation of pretending to be like our son by doing a big histrionic show in order to hide the same frustration that we all feel about this horrible reality of being dominated by a foreign nation. Just like Guaraguao, some Puerto Ricans have confronted the American Empire by using the wrong mechanisms. Guaraguao, again, is a vivid example of some belligerent wrong actions. He uses our little son as a mechanism of defense to project himself as a warrior and to wrongly represent the great courage of our little Pitirre, small but with a lion heart. Everyone knows that in the face of adversity, Pitirre does not step backwards to defend what he believes is the right thing.

Mrs. Pitirre: What are we going to do, then? Have you read the psychologist's reports where he states that our son suffers from a learning disability? His diagnosis reflects a severe case, and he recommends placing our dear son in Self Contained Classes; furthermore, he prescribed him some strong drugs to improve his behavior.

Mr. Pitirre: Let me have a deep breath and count to one hundred! O.K. Look, Sweetheart. You know better than anybody else that Pitirre is not retarded; the only individuals that are mentally challenged are all of those who think that our son is mentally subpar.

Mrs. Pitirre: What are we going to do, then? Pitirre has been locked in his bedroom for two consecutive days, and he does not want to come out. I only know that he is alive by his dreadful dreams when he loudly repeats that he does not want to speak English.

Mr. Pitirre: Our last trip together was salutary; he did not suffer from calamitous dreams. He was very gregarious and garrulous; in fact, he did not interact with anybody interested in ruining his happiness. We'll take him on a trip for several days in order to ameliorate his stressful condition.

Mrs. Pitirre: I agree with you. I hope he changes and gets to be the same he used to be; if not, I am the one that is going to become crazy.

Pitirre: *(Composing some verses in his dreams)*

I used to be nice;
I used to be humble.
I used to dream over you
every minute of my life.

I used to be true;
I used to be good.
I used to think of you
every second of my life.

I used to go farther;
I used to love you
like no one in this world
could've loved you before.

Today, you are not
in my heart anymore,
and I still think
that it wasn't my fault.

Mr. Pitirre: Son, pack it up; we are going on a trip, but this time your mother is coming with us.

Mrs. Pitirre: *(Inside her son's bedroom)* I am going to help you pack. What are you going to take?

Pitirre: First of all, I'd like to take my storybooks.

Mrs. Pitirre: Don't take them all. Just take three of your favorite ones.

Pitirre: Wow! That is a difficult task. OK. I will take: "The Incredible Adventures of Oink Oink, the Little Pig", "The Incredible Adventures of Baa Baa, the Little Goat", and "The Incredible Adventures of Ribbit Ribbit, the Little Frog".

Mrs. Pitirre: Fantastic! Everything is all set. I'm very excited about this trip.

Mr. Pitirre: I am ready, too. I can't wait to spend a few days visiting some old friends. Let's go.

Pitirre: *(Talking to himself)* It is about time that my parents take me out. This is going to be an unforgettable trip.

Once again under the blue sky of Borinquén, Pitirre was flying blithely, but this time with the company of both of his parents.

Pitirre: Daddy! What a cool and windy morning! Look at the magnanimous green mountains from up here.

Mr. Pitirre: Yes. The climate on our island is temperate in December; the air is redolent of wood smoke and aromatic flowers.

Mrs. Pitirre: Yes. Our island is a paragon of beauty.

Pitirre: Look, Daddy. Look at the contrasting white color of the waves with the blue of the pristine sea! It seems that the waves are being rushed, and they are eager to arrive to the white sandy beaches to perfume and cover them with their fragrant foam.

Mr. Pitirre: A very poetic observation, Son!

Pitirre: By the way, when are you going to recite to us a romantic poem?

Mrs. Pitirre: Come on, please our son. I also would love to listen to one of your unique lyric poems.

Mr. Pitirre: You really know that poetry is my weakness. I am very contented you enjoy my anachronistic practice of reciting poems.

Mrs. Pitirre: Let us rest under that palm tree and drink some water from its coconuts, what do you think?

Pitirre: Brilliant suggestion! Daddy will also recite one of those impressive poems he used to declaim to you before he married you, Mom.

Mrs. Pitirre: I think that's a marvelous idea.

Mr. Pitirre: *(Looking at his son)* Listen to my favorite poem that I recited to your mother when my eyes met hers for the first time:

I would like to be the day
or perhaps its light,
so I could illuminate
your walking through path.

I would like to be the moon
or perhaps a star,
so I could illuminate
your alluring silhouette.

I would like to be the flame
that turns your heart on
and in moonless nights
illuminate your balcony.

I would like to be the poet
who in love composes
sweet verses of love
on the constellations.

I would like to be the lighthouse
that illuminates from afar,
so I could guide your wishes
throughout my kisses.

I would like to be the breeze
at the edge of the sea,
for I could whisper to you
a very special song.

I would like to be from the river,
the coolest current,
and announce our love
to the whole world.

I would like to be the sailboat
that navigates in your heart,
and founder in your chest
as the compass of a watch.

I would like to be the dew
in the cool morning
and refresh your love and mine
at the bottom of my soul.

I would like to be from the flowers
the coolest fragrance
and to satiate with my lips
all your anxieties.

I would like to be the tone
composed by my harp
and to record your glowing eyes
in my sweet songs.

I would like to be the bird
that happily delivers
unforgettable notes of love
to the hearts.

I would like to be the air
that you breathe every second,
so I can travel your body
from your head to your toes.

I would like to be from the ocean
the most fragrant foam
to bathe your private domains
under the moon light.

I would like to be the summer
or may be its light,
so I can melt in your body
and cover it with love.

I would like to be that tree
of the forbidden fruit
to cover with its leaves
your body and mine.

All of those things and more
I would like to become
and in every instant of my life
deliver them to you all.

Pitirre: Lovely! Dad! You are the greatest. I have always liked to listen to you reciting poems to my mother. When I grow up, I will declaim poems like you.

Mr. Pitirre: *(Looking at his wife)* Why are you crying?

Mrs. Pitirre: I am not crying. These are just tears of excitement. Waves of nostalgia overcome me every time I listen to that poem; I feel the same vibrations as when my eyes met yours for the first time, too.

Pitirre: Awesome! That is my Mom! I have such a romantic mother. Well! We have had enough rest, and it is time to continue our trip. Don't you agree?

Mrs. Pitirre: I do not see any inconvenience.

Mr. Pitirre: Neither do I. What do you think if we go to El Verde and spend some time there, later, we can visit Luquillo and have some fun at the beach?

Pitirre: Awesome! Do you like his idea, Mom?

Mrs. Pitirre: It's terrific! There are a lot of small stores with Puerto Rican typical dishes. They sell excellent piononos which are some kind of ripe plantains stuff with ground beef; I love them.

Pitirre: Pionono! Yes. I have heard about that dish. I'd love to try it, too.

Mr. Pitirre: I'm resolute to eat a combination of yellow rice and crab meat, six crab tacos, five potatoes stuff with ground beef, ten beef patties, and some fried codfish; moreover, I will have a dessert made out of coconut and some cinnamon powder on top; I will also drink the water of three ice cold coconuts and...

Scene Three

The Pitirres fly one more time across the limpid blue sky of Puerto Rico and reached the exuberant green mountains of El Verde where they relaxed and spent a memorable time. Later, they all went to swim in the crystal clear and warm waters of Luquillo Beach.

Mr. Pitirre: We have swum enough, and I'm getting hungry. How about if we go and eat?

Mrs. Pitirre: That's fine with me but be careful. Just do not forget what happened to you when you visited my sister in Mayaguez.

Pitirre: Yes, Dad. If you eat too much, you may end up having diarrhea, again.

Mr. Pitirre: All right. I'll try not being a glutton.

Each one orders their favorite typical dishes. Pitirre's mother reminds her husband not to eat so much; all are satisfied and discuss the next place to visit.

Pitirre: *(Involved in his thoughts)* How wonderful! We will travel to Loíza Aldea, Piñones, Isla Verde, and Punta Las Marías. I will probably be able to see my friend, the one who lives in *Lloréns.*

The Pitirres make a short stop at Lloréns Torres in order to say hello to some old friends. Pitirre has the opportunity to play with his friend for a little while. An unparalleled pink and orange sunset shows up in the horizon of the blue sky of the Enchanted Island. The Pitirres say good bye to their friends; and then, continue their trip to the Old San Juan where they make another short stop at the Ashford Avenue in The Condado area.

Mr. Pitirre: The beef patties we ate at our friends' house were delicious.

Pitirre: I liked the croquettes stuffed with ham.

Mrs. Pitirre: Everything was luscious.

Mr. Pitirre: The sugar cane juice was delectable, also.

Mrs. Pitirre: Are you sure you were drinking sugar cane juice? I bet you and your friend were drinking Pitorro, instead.

Pitirre: Dad. Why didn't you give me some Pitorro? Mom, what is Pitorro?

Mrs. Pitirre: It is a home-made fermented beverage but don't worry about it. That is business for...

Pitirre: *(Interrupting his mother)* I know. It is business for adults.

Mr. Pitirre: What a traffic jam! I thought traffic jams were found only in Bayamon, but this is even worse. It is incredible. Let's stop on top of that penthouse to contemplate the view.

Mrs. Pitirre: Oh, I know that in Bayamón and at the Baldority de Castro Avenue there are traffic jams due to the working schedules. It is almost 8:00 p.m., and there is no reason to have this type of jams at the Ashford Avenue.

Mr. Pitirre: Since this is a tourist area, there is always activity twenty-four hours a day; many youngsters like to waste their time just by circulating around without making a stop.

Pitirre: This is spectacular! I will do the same when I grow up.

Mr. Pitirre: *(Looking at his wife)* Would you like to drink a Piña Colada in this hotel?

Mrs. Pitirre: No, thanks. Not here. I would love to have it in Old San Juan, instead.

Mr. Pitirre: We may find a traffic jam, as well, but I know what you mean. Down there, we will really feel in Puerto Rico. This Condado area with its luxurious hotels seems to be a precarious copy of some of the tourist areas of our unwanted American protector. When we get there, I will let Pitirre try a Virgin Piña Colada; I'm sure he is going to love it.

Scene Four

Students Choir: *Wake up Borinqueño. The signal has been given! Wake up from that dream because it is time to...*

Pitirre and Guaraguao return to school after a protracted suspension from school.

Mr. Owl: Majestic! Remarkable! I told you that you were geniuses. There is no doubt; I have the most melodious and sophisticated voices of the entire island. Congratulations! You represent the greatest pride of our country.

Guaraguao: *(To the teacher)* Did you remember that you were going to tell us why you have decorated this classroom using green and white colors?

Mr. Owl: Yes. I haven't forgotten. In fact, let me tell you right now. The white color represents peace; peace in which all of us would like to live in. Peace represents freedom; we cannot have peace without freedom. Yes. Freedom means to air our flag along with other nations, to proudly sing our national anthem along with other countries, to posses our own currency without stamped images on it of leaders from a foreign land, to do business with any republic without fetter imperialist governments circumscribing restrictions to our personal freedoms. *(All the students clapped with fervor to the teacher; there are tears coming out from their eyes.)* The green symbolizes life. It is the color of our mountains: the fecundity of our land. You are that fertility; you represent the life and future of our land. We cannot allow foreign forces to own and dominate our lives; we have enough with the natural forces such as the hurricanes that arrive every year and threaten us. I could continue telling you more about it, but time is gold, and our class is about music and not civics.

Mr. Owl's polemic speech was so compelling that the students frenetically lauded him and even the dogmatic teacher had tears coming out from his sad eyes this time.

Pitirre: The truth is that our preeminent teacher really knows how to use figurative language to convey his pellucid message; he has a highly developed aesthetic sense. His succinct explanation was astonishingly persuadable and did not compromise himself talking politically; however, he did it poetically. He was cogent in explaining the meaning of the white and green colors.

We all understood him perspicuously enough; I want to be as doctrinaire as him when I grow up.

Pitirre and Coquí exited the school. It's a cloudy and humid afternoon.

Coquí: I think we have rehearsed enough for the monumental play that Mr. Owl has programmed for this Christmas. Don't you agree?

Pitirre: Definitely. That is so. In fact, I believe that Mr. Owl should start sending home the parents' invitations.

Coquí: Stop. Don't walk. I think I saw something moving behind those trees; I have the feeling that we are being watched.

Pitirre: From whom and for what?

Coquí: I don't know. Let's keep on walking.

Pitirre: Yes. Let's walk. Oh! I forgot to tell you that I only need to translate eight more words to finish my homework for tomorrow, a poem dedicated to my beloved Puerto Rico. It goes like this:

A point on the mar.
Yes, that's what you are.
Oh, my dear Puerto Rico!
My land of the palmar.

You are the place of my dreams—
a place of immense verdor,
and I won't take anymore
than your bello splendor.

Your beaches serenas
tranquil and bellas
resemble the eyes
of my Borinqueña:
The only one that
takes away my penas.

Pitirre: *(After a long walk)* Well, we are getting close to our homes. I guess you were exaggerating.

Coquí: Perhaps but I could swear that somebody was watching us; you can come to my house later, so we can do our homework together.

Pitirre: *(Pitirre hurries to his home and from the distance answers to his friend.)* All right, I will let my mom know about it. Ouch!

Coquí: *(Talking to himself)* What was that? I think I heard a cry coming from the same direction taken by Pitirre; I will find out. I have the sensation that something wrong could've happened to him. Oh, no! Pitirre, Pitirre. What are you doing lying on the ground? Come on. Get up. He doesn't answer; he is unconscious, or maybe he is dead. Who could've harmed him? *(Coquí looks around him and* *discovers a trace of dried leaves recently broken by footsteps. Cautiously, he tries to reach to some bushes nearby, but before he gets there, he listens to the noise of some birds' wings flying away in a hurry.)* This is an idiosyncratic situation. What should I do? If he is not dead, and I go ask for help; the ones that made the desultory attempt to kill him may return to finish him. If he is dead, they would not be able to do anymore harm than what they already did. What a dilemma! I can't stay here; I am going to look for help. I'll go to his house; I am sure his mother will be there.

Coquí arrives to Pitirre's house and with a high tone in his voice starts calling his parents.

Mrs. Pitirre: Gee! What's all that yelling! Has anybody been killed?

Coquí: Yes. I mean, no. The truth is that I don't know. It's your son. He is lying down on the road; he is unresponsive. Hurry up. Let's find out what's going on with him. We are probably still in time to save his life.

Mrs. Pitirre: I don't understand; he was fine when I left him at the school this morning.

Mr. Pitirre: Listen, what's the hurry?

Coquí: It's your son, Mr. Pitirre. Something wrong has happened to him; there is no time to waste. Let's get him. If we hurry, maybe we could still save his life.

Mr. Pitirre: Then, this is serious.

Coquí: *(Arriving to the place)* It's here. Look at him. He's right there. He still is in the same position as when I left him; he hasn't moved at all.

Mr. Pitirre: He is unconscious. Hurry! Let's take him to the Medical Center, so he can be taken care of. I can't understand what could've happened.

Coquí: In other words, he is still breathing. He's alive!

Mr. Pitirre: Yes. He probably hit something that made him fall down.

Coquí: What was that?

Mr. Pitirre: What?

Mrs. Pitirre: *(Pointing at some bushes)* I heard a noise coming from overthere; I think someone is hiding.

Coquí: I'm scared.

Mr. Pitirre: Don't be afraid. I am here. It's getting dark. Let's hurry, on the contrary, he is not going to survive.

Scene Five

Coquí is in the Emergency Room at the Medical Center in Río Piedras. He narrates in chronological order the sequence of events to the police; he also answers some questions about possible suspects that could have perpetrated the horrible action of harming his best friend. The investigators leave the hospital in search of the potential suspects. A few minutes later, Coquí's parents arrive to the hospital to pick up their son. Meantime, Pitirre's parents have been desperately waiting for more than five hours for the physician's diagnosis.

Mr. Pitirre: I wonder what's happening inside that room. I feel my blood pressure getting high.

Mrs. Pitirre: *(With an apprehensive attitude)* I don't know. I am concerned; we have been waiting here for a long time.

Pitirre: *(Unconscious inside the emergency room)* I am cold. I want to be with my mom. Where's my dad? Where are my friends? Why have you forsaken me? I feel very lonely. It's dark; there isn't a single star tonight. I feel like I am floating in the darkness.

Mrs. Pitirre: I have the feeling that our son wants to communicate with us.

Pitirre: I can't move. What is happening to me? Am I going to die? Don't leave me here, please. I don't want to die; I haven't finished translating my poem for tomorrow's homework. Mom. Mom. Dad. Dad. Oh, no! I cannot believe what I'm looking at:

There's my coffin! There, it is!
Gray. Sad. Cold.
Gray, sad, and cold like my soul:
Without a sunrise; without a sunset.

A teardrop may fall down. Perhaps!
It may fall down on top of it. Perhaps!
A teardrop that will warm
the cold darkness of the night.

Or perhaps no one will remember,
after a few days,
who lies inside,
inside of its walls.

My coffin soon will be locked!
A pity flower someone will throw
symbolizing a trip:
A trip to the land of solitude.

The cemetery silently sleeps now.
A new guest lives there,
inside a gray, sad, and cold coffin;
as cold as the night...

Meantime at the police station, one of the suspects is being interrogated by a trenchant detective.

Bow Wow: Tell me. Is it true or is it not true that you kept on annoying Pitirre?

Guaraguao: Yes. It's true.

Bow Wow: Tell me. Is it true or is it not true that you were disseminating a rumor stating that Pitirre was crazy?

Guaraguao: Yes. It's true.

Bow Wow: Tell me, is it true or is it not true that you ate pork chops early this afternoon?

Guaraguao: Yes. It's true. How do you know that?

Bow Wow: Shut up. I am the one that asks the questions here. Tell me is it true or is it not true that you and your gang were surreptitiously hanging around at the Maravilla Mountain where Pitirre's body was found lying right on the ground?

Guaraguao: Yes. It is true.

Bow Wow: You are under arrest while we finish doing our investigation.

Guaraguao: I request a good for nothing counselor; I mean a crook with a license to lie. I haven't transgressed the law.

Bow Wow: Do you mean a liar or a lawyer?

Guaraguao: Aren't they the same thing?

The surgeon calls Pitirre's parents and asks them to be strong. He tells them that their son is in a coma and living his last minutes.

Mrs. Pitirre: *(Crying)* It can't be. This is not fair. It can't be. Why him? Why him? It's not fair. He is so little! God, take me as a surrogate for my son.

Mr. Pitirre: Be strong. Be strong. I know it's not fair. I would also give my life to save him; he is the noblest creature I have ever met. It's not fair.

Pitirre: *(Recovering consciousness and sighing for his last time)* I don't want to speak English. I don't want to sp...

Mr. Pitirre: *(Crying aloud)* NOO. NOOOOOOOO. NOOOOOO. NOOOOOOOOOO. *(He fell down as struck by a thunder)*

Mrs. Pitirre: *(yelling in despair)* Doctor. Doctor. Hurry up. Come and check my husband, please.

Doctor: *(Examines Mr. Pitirre)* I am sorry. Your husband is dead; his heart could not resist the strain.

Mrs. Pitirre: *(Crying)* Noooooooo. Nooooooo. Noooo. Noooo. What about my son, doctor? I heard him mumbling.

Doctor: *(Examines Pitirre)* I am sorry. He is dead, too.

Mrs. Pitirre: *(Whipping)* Doctor. What was the cause of my son's death?

Doctor: The blood test has shown evidence of high concentration of radioactivity in his lungs and in his digestive tract system. Was your son on the island of Vieques, by any chance?

Mrs. Pitirre: Yes. He and his father were there. I remember that my husband commented once about the painful stomach ache that our son suffered after eating a lot of cherry azaroles.

Doctor: There is the answer. The U.S. Air Force has vitiated the air in Vieques; eating anything from that island is deleterious to anybody's health, so those contaminated cherry azaroles plus the noxious air pollution were the bane agents for their existence.

Mrs. Pitirre: No wonder! Pitirre was not the same. He started losing his appetite; on the other hand, my husband was suffering from painful stomach aches and diarrhea. I wouldn't ever have thought that those symptoms were a portent of a tragic ending.

Doctor: Your husband was a strong adult, but he would have died in the same way.

Mrs. Pitirre: Oh! I am bereaved. Why do we have to suffer, and why do we have to pay in this way?

Doctor: That is the putative question. It is time for all of us to wake up once and for all and to look at the vitriolic actions committed against our land in order to preclude tragedies like these.

Mrs. Pitirre:

It's too hard to believe
after so much love
that you aren't
with me anymore.

After so many hugs...
After so much love...
Tell me, where my life
is going to go?

It's too hard to believe
after so many dreams
that they have destroyed
the castle and its king.

It's too hard to believe
after so many dreams
that they have destroyed
the castle and its prince.

It's too hard to believe
after so many nights
that half of my life,
I've lost it tonight.

On a dark and cloudy afternoon, the funerals are held.
Educators, students, friends, and members of the community
were attending in order to give their last respects.

Mr. Guaraguao: Son. A chapter ends today and a new one opens up in our lives. This has been a big lesson for us.

Guaraguao: I know. It is a poignant situation to see the departure of a friend. It makes me feel bad just to think that I never valued his friendship; however, it never crossed my mind to harm him in anyway. I am glad my claim of innocence has been vindicated.

Mr. Guaraguao: That is why I affirm that this is a big lesson for all of us. Most of the time we don't appreciate what we have until we lose it, and when we do, it is already too late.

Guaraguao: Like in this case.

Mr. Guaraguao: Yes, indeed.

Guaraguao: *(Thinking)*

"You belong to one world;
I belong to another
very different than yours",
you told me once.

Life is funny; I believe.
It teaches us something new
every time we don't expect.

It teaches us how to love
and how to care;
to whom our heart
we have to give,
so Pitirre don't be scared;
you have won my respect.

Sun of Borinquén: I feel so sad. I cannot excuse myself
by not being with Pitirre in his last moments…

Not every night, one has the privilege
to watch a comet traveling through the sky,
bringing with its brilliance
good messages to Earth.

As our ancestors used to say,
"Once you have the fortune to see it;
you will never forget its glow."

So it has been you, Pitirre,
who has traveled through
fields of love,
delivering your kindness
and tender advices to our hearts.

We will never forget you
because like a comet
you also shine
yet with a difference;
you also shine inside.

Silver Moon: I feel very sorry for the bereft widow who is beset by grief at this time. Everything would have been differently, perhaps, if I would have come out a little earlier to make a round-watch by the mountain…

A plaintive song by Coquí is heard that lugubrious night:

He finally rested;
no more voices were heard.
In peace, he will be,
with no more reproaches.

He never understood
so much cruelty,
from a mercilessly world
that never appreciated him.

He gave out a lot of love;
he got none in return.
In this way, he left
carrying a deep pain.

He was always silent
waiting for a hug,
yet he was condemned
of getting none at all.

His laments were heard
while agonizing;
it was his soul crying
before departing to the cemetery.

He wept for the ones left behind—
for his beloved ones.
"I don't want to speak English",
He repeated in his agony.

It happened; fair it was.
He ran away from humankind.
He will now live, forever and ever,
in eternal grace.

Relatives and friends,
he wouldn't see anymore.
Between rumors and laments
he was welcomed in the graveyard.

Little by little everyone left;
little by little, they walked away.
There was nothing else to do;
no one would see him again.

Lonely, as he came to the world;
lonely, he left too.
Lonely, very lonely,
leaving an open wound
very deep in our souls.

Three months later. On a bright and lively morning, an angelic lullaby song is heard.

Mrs. Pitirre: *Rock-A-Bye Baby in the Tree Top-When the Wind Blows the Cradle Will Rock…*Hum! It seems to me that you'd like to listen to a different song. All right, I will improvise one especially for you…

*You came into my life
right on time
when I needed you most,
making my sadness
go away,
making my hopes
grow more.*

*You awoke my feelings
for love;
you awoke my feelings
for you;
you filled my world
with happiness
and tenderness
with something special
known as love.*

Look at you. You really look like your father: Same eyes, same cheeks, same hands, same fingers, same legs…

Sun of Borinquén: I don't think so. I think he looks like Pitirre.

Silver Moon: I think he looks like both.

End

Books written by the author

Short story *(Bilingual Spanish/English)*

The Incredible Adventures of Pew Pew, the Little Chicken
The Incredible Adventures of Kluck Kluck, the Little Hen
The Incredible Adventures of Cock-A-Doodle-Do, the Little Rooster
The Incredible Adventures of Kuack Kuack, the Little Duck
The Incredible Adventures of Oink Oink, the Little Pig
The Incredible Adventures of Bow Wow, the Little Dog
The Incredible Adventures of Meow Meow, the Little Cat
The Incredible Adventures of Baa Baa, the Little Goat
The Incredible Adventures of Moo Moo, the Little Cow
The Incredible Adventures of Ribbit Ribbit, the Little Frog
The Incredible Adventures of Baaa, Baaa, the Little Lamb
The Incredible Adventures of Maa Maa, the Little Calf
The Incredible Adventures of Kroack Kroack, the Little Toad
The Incredible Adventures of Coqui
The Incredible Adventures of Pancho

Poetry *(Spanish)*

Simplemente tú y yo
Secretos
Añoranza
Ensueño (Antología poética)

Drama

PITIRRE DOES NOT WANT TO SPEAK ENGLISH
PITIRRE NO QUIERE HABLAR INGLÉS (Spanish Version)

Libros escritos por el autor

Poesía:

01. Simplemente tú y yo
02. Secretos
03. Añoranza
04. Ensueño (Antología poética)

Cuento:

01. Las increíbles aventuras del cochinito Oink Link
02. Las increíbles aventuras del sapito Kroak Kroak
03. Las increíbles aventuras de la vaquita Muú Muú
04. Las increíbles aventuras de la ranita Ribet Ribet
05. Las increíbles aventuras de la gatita Miau Miau
06. Las increíbles aventuras del perrito Guau Guau
07. Las increíbles aventuras del becerrito Meé Meé
08. Las increíbles aventuras de la gallinita Kló Kló
09. Las increíbles aventuras del patito Kuak Kuak
10. Las increíbles aventuras de la chivita Beé Beé
11. Las increíbles aventuras del gallito Kikirikí
12. Las increíbles aventuras del pollito Pío Pío
13. Las increíbles aventuras del Coquí
14. Las increíbles aventuras de Pancho

Drama:

Pitirre no quiere hablar inglés